My Journey Wasn't Easy

From Farm to City to an International Career

Jean Moore Fasse

Edited by
Charles R. George, Ph.D.

Chapel Hill Press, Inc.

ISBN Number   1-880849-33-x
Library of Congress Catalog   2001090597

Manufactured in the United States of America
05 04 03 02 01   10 9 8 7 6 5 4 3 2

Table of Contents

Introduction

Life on the Farm.. 1

Elementary School Days............................. 15

The Community 19

High School Days 23

Teaching Career 37

India 47

France & Germany 61

Czechoslovakia... 67

Moscow 83

Appendix 99

Introduction

After returning to America from Germany in 1990, I found that I had a lot of free time on my hands. One day while just sitting around looking through different magazines, it dawned on me that maybe I should try to write my life story. I started writing, but then my eyes began to fail me and I could not continue, so I just stopped all together. One day a lady from the Blind Assistance Program came by to assist me, and show me how I could do things for myself. As we started talking about different places I had been, traveling and so forth, she said it seemed as if I had a very interesting story to tell, since I had done a lot of traveling around the world. Then she asked me if I had ever thought about taping the story of my life. I began to think about this very seriously, so I decided to start from my childhood and culminate with the accomplishments I had made in my life.

The story of my life includes my early childhood, education, profession, and travels. This story is dedicated to: Betsy Stuart, an assistant director in Radio Reading Service for the Blind, who I met through a blind assistance program. Being legally blind myself, had it not been for Betsy, I never would have written my story. Having no one to assist me in this project and after hearing some of my story, she encouraged me to tape it. Since I could not see how to write it, she assisted me all the way. I started at eighty-nine years old, and now at ninety and-a-half years old, I have finished it.

In retrospect, my biography reminds me that:

> *If you want to be happy for a day,*
> *lend a helping hand.*
> *If you want to be happy for a lifetime,*
> *teach a child to learn and dream.*

My life has been full of many interesting experiences. Because I was born during the years of segregation, trying to advance in life was very difficult for me. I have enjoyed the chance to travel, work, and live abroad for many years. As I remembered these adventures, I decided to tell the story of my life, in the hope that my story may inspire our youth to continue to get an education, in spite of hardships, disadvantages, and other adverse conditions that may arise. To adults, I hope it will kindle memories of similar experiences from their past.

Life On The Farm

s I look back on my early childhood in rural
Lillington, North Carolina, my first memories
are before I could talk. As I lay on a palate in
a room by the window, I saw three white geese or
birds that flew to the window, paused and kept
going. As I could not talk, I could not tell anyone
about this, but it always stayed in my mind. When
it was so that I could talk and spoke about it, someone said that it was only a dream. It was not a
dream.

I was born third child of eight, named Mamie
Jane Moore. We lived in a small community where
whites and blacks lived in close proximity to each
other. My father was highly respected. His name
was John the Baptist Moore, but he was called the
Reverend Moore by the blacks and Baptist Moore or

Uncle Baptist by whites. One day, as a white man came in the store which was owned and operated by my father, he said in a friendly tone, "Howdy Uncle Baptist." I was only five years old but I looked up at him and said, "My Papa's not your uncle. He's black and you are white." They got a laugh out of it, but my father was disturbed and sent me out of the store. At the evening meal all the little things that the children did, and could get punished for, were discussed. My father spoke about this and I said to myself, "I'm going to get a whoopen." I just know he is going to say something. I said, "Papa, you are highly respected and the black people call you Reverend Moore but the white people call you Baptist or Uncle Baptist. Why is that?" He looked at my mother, whose name was Frances, and he said, "Frances you talk to that gal, she is getting very ornery." I always did ask a lot of questions, but never got answers. As I grew older, I found out that he really didn't have the answers to give me.

My father was the seventh child of twenty-six. Not being able to attend school but for one or two months of the year, he taught himself to read. He learned to read the Bible very well. Three of his brothers also became preachers. They all lived at home until they were twenty-one. They all were also

farmers. I often wondered why there were so many preachers in his family. I came up with the answer. It was because there was no place for them to go but to church. Everyone went to church on Sundays and also during the week. The highlight of the year was the revival meeting. People would stop their work in the middle of the day to go to revival. The pastor would call people to the mourner's bench. They would get on their knees, cry, roll around, sing and clap until they got religion. When they got up and jumped around they were supposed to have gotten religion. I sang a lot in church. When I was around twelve years old my father said it was time for me to get religion. I never understood this type of thing, but one afternoon at the revival, I got on my knees, prayed and tried to cry. Nothing came. So I decided to get up and shout around a little bit to make them think I had religion. I believe in God and always have, but I don't think I got religion there on my knees. On Sundays, we would always go to church and stay most of the day. We had to leave home one hour earlier to get there on time because we went by wagon or walked. Sunday School was at 9:00 a.m. and preaching began at 11:00 a.m. and lasted until 1:00 or 1:30 p.m. The pastor never knew when to sit down. After service,

they would take up collection where everyone had to walk around and show off their new clothes and put their money on the table. After this was finished, big tables were set up outside. All the food was placed on them and the people ate all they wanted. We would get home around 3:00 p.m. We had to attend Sunday school, whether it was cold, raining, or snowing. Today I do not attend anybody's Sunday school. I feel that I have gone through all the Sunday school lessons that I need. My uncle was one of the main preachers for the revival season. He could get everyone in the community to come to church. He liked to use a little firewater, as they called it. The little sip would give him more spirit, I suppose. My uncle would take his little bottle to church. He would go to the door, take a little sip and then come back. Everyone would go to the mourners' bench. There was much singing. The people could really sing. The white people would come and stand around outside and listen to the singing going on in the church. Lots of times they were invited to come in and listen to the service. They also had revival meetings. When they came to our church, they were given the seats in the front, but when we visited their church, we would have to sit in the back. We could hardly hear what was going on;

therefore, we did not attend their church very much.

My grandfather, Anthony Moore, lived to be one hundred and ten years old. He worked on his little peanut farm until the day he died. Sitting in a small chair going from patch to patch, working with his peanuts, was what he was doing when he died.

I'd like to speak a little more about my family and my childhood as I was growing up, over seventy-five years ago. There were many things that we grew on the farm, but there were also many things that we didn't like to eat. Now hominy grits were different from the type of grits that you have today. It was something like the grain in the corn, and I don't know exactly just how they prepared it, but it had a different taste that we never liked. My father would always say that if we ate hominy grits, we would grow up to be very pretty and have long, silky hair. This was something that all young girls wanted to have. Maybe he said that because the silks in the corn were long and silky. However, because of our genes, we could never have had that kind of hair. Another food was beef that you could get with the white gristles in it. Having eight children (nine with an adopted daughter) in the family, it was necessary to stretch beef for everybody to have an ample share.

Although we lived in the segregated south, we were not raised to think that we were inferior to the whites. However, it seemed to us as children that we were inferior because we did not have things the white children had. My father would tell us, "Okay, now these gristles are very, very good. If you eat these gristles you will become white." Of course we would chew, chew, and chew on these gristles but we could never chew them up. There came a time that I began thinking that these gristles were not making anybody white. Miss Patty was a white lady who came to my father's store. My mother would always be outside washing in the big black wash pot while her daughter, Jenny, and I made sand pies and mud pies together. Miss Patty would go inside and walk around the store and talk with my mother before she would buy anything. I never knew what they were talking about. One day while Miss Patty was shopping around, I asked Jenny, "Do you eat many gristles?" She said, "What are gristles?" and I said, "White gristles that you get from eating beef. You're white, did the gristles make you white?" She said, "No." She didn't know anything about anybody getting white by eating gristles. So, I found out that my father's information about gristles was wrong. Jenny stopped coming by to play. I

never found out why she didn't come anymore. One day my mother and I were in town and we saw Miss Patty. My mother spoke and said, "Hello, Miss Patty." She just said, "Hi, Frances," and kept going. I said, "Hello," to Jenny and she did not speak to me. I asked my mother why they didn't speak. She said, "Now you are growing up and you will go your way, and she will go hers." This was the only way that they knew how to explain segregation at that time.

I knew my father and mother loved us, but I have never known a time when my father put his arms around me. I've never seen my father show any affection for my mother. I never saw him put his hand on her shoulder or around her, but I believe they did the best they knew, and always provided for us. This affected the children, especially the boys, because I noticed that my brothers did not show affections for their wives as men should, but they were always good to them. I never felt anything against my parents because I felt that was the only way that they knew how to do things. I loved them and I believe that they loved me. Although I did not have the same affection for my father as I did for my mother. It seemed that my father felt that I should always stay around and work on the farm. If he were here today, I'm sure he would be

pleased with the progress I have made.

Unlike children going to school today who have many choices of the different types of food they want to eat, we had to take lunch, which consisted of what we had at home. Looking back, I remember taking a little bucket with syrup, biscuits or cornbread, and fatback meat. Many days, I did not take lunch because I didn't want to eat what we had. There was a store not far from the school. Candy didn't cost what it does now. A big Baby Ruth only cost five cents, so to get extra money to stop by the store, I would dig up stumps around the farm. Living on a farm, we had lots of little stumps and my father would give us five cents for every one we dug up. I would get up early in the morning and go out looking for stumps. When I found one, I would dig it up with a shovel or axe. I would take it and show it to my father so I could get my money to buy candy. That would mostly be my lunch until I got back home, and then we would have supper; usually peas, collards, cabbage or whatever was there. We seemed to thrive and be very healthy under those conditions.

My father could have been a very successful man because he was a hard worker, and taught us to work hard. All farmers didn't get the same price at

the tobacco market for tobacco sold. The blacks got a lot less than the whites for their farm products. I remember when they would go to the tobacco market we would work all night, working with the tobacco to keep it at the right temperature. Although my father made a good grade of tobacco, he still didn't get top price when it was sold. We used to pick cotton. When it rained and we couldn't pick cotton we would sit in the tobacco barn and help grade tobacco. My father would take the tobacco to Fuquay Springs, North Carolina, for sale. Although the tobacco was pretty and tied neatly in stacks, the price was always lower than for the white man. It was the same way at the cotton sale. We worked hard picking cotton, baled it, and took it to the market, but we never made top price. And I could really pick cotton. I would pick over four hundred pounds per day. My father made a little progress during that time because we had a house that burned and evidently my father had insurance on it, because the next house we moved in was better than the old one. The old one had holes in the floor and wind would come up through them. The only heat we had was the fireplace. Of course, the front of your legs got warmed and burned, but you never could get warm all over. My father tried to buy

everything that came his way. When he went to the tobacco market and came back with money, and the white men knew he had gotten paid, they would bring things over to sell, and he would buy them. He bought things I don't think he really needed. Because of this he got in debt. It was as though my father trusted everybody. My father would let people buy things on credit and they would not pay him. He didn't keep receipts. When I grew up and went to college, I'd come home on weekends to help my father. The same kinds of things were still happening at the store. Every Monday, people would bring in leftover bread from what they didn't use over the weekend to exchange. I would be in the store and notice people bringing in bread and other things and just put them down and come back and tell my father he owed them "so and so" and he could pay them.

I would tell my father that he had no receipts to show who brought what in, because he didn't see what they bought in the store, but he would say to me, "I know what I'm doing". I trust these people. I've been here working with these people all this long time. Don't come here trying to start any trouble." I was just trying to say that he should have kept receipts so he could see what was happening.

He never would do it and owed a man one thousand dollars, which he paid. But when my father died, my sister and everybody in the family had to get together and pay it back because he didn't keep the receipts.

Papa loved white people because they were not all distrustful of him, and he loved everybody. There are good people and distrustful people in every race and you will find this to be true as you go through life. Bad things happened to me as I grew up, but I never became bitter, because some people didn't think or just didn't notice when they did these things.

I remember statements that I've heard a lot of them say. If something comes up regarding race, a common expression was, "I have a lot of black friends," and some of them did. I can honestly say that I have several white friends that I would go down for because they have stuck with me as well as anybody else. And of course in the home there were four girls and four boys. I was the third child, and there were several born after I was.

As soon as we were able to walk we had to meet in a room every morning. Papa had prayer every morning at 4:00 a.m. and if you could walk, everyone had to get out of bed and be there. When every-

body got there and got on their knees, my father would go along with this long prayer that I'm quite sure others didn't understand, and I didn't understand it myself because I would go to sleep. Of course I would get many little spankings because when the prayer was over I would be asleep.

And as we grew up, my mother said it was time for us to learn to cook because breakfast had to be ready by 5:00 a.m. for the men to go in the fields and do the plowing or whatever they had to do to get ready for the farm. My older sister would cook one week and I would cook the next week. This was something I did not want to do. I didn't want to learn to cook or even get up that early in the morning. I would always be sleepy. So when my time came to learn to cook, I was to make biscuits, because I had seen how they were supposed to be done. I either put too much grease or flour, and when they tried to eat them, they would complain because I would always mess up the food. We usually had syrup, and fat back meat along with the biscuits.

Because I kept my fingernails long, my brothers decided they didn't want to eat my cooking because my fingernails were not clean. Of course I kept them long to get out of cooking. I didn't mind doing

anything outside in the fields or anything else other than cooking. So then they stopped me from cooking. I was glad. They didn't know they did me a favor. That's why I had to do all the work in the fields. My sisters learned to be very good cooks, but I never did.

My parents, Rev. John "The Baptist" Moore and Lilly Francis Moore.
Authors Private Collection (APC)

Elementary School Days

I started school at seven years old and walked five miles daily through the woods to a one-room schoolhouse where children in the community of all ages attended. Classes were set up for different ages. I was not afraid because there were other children along the way and houses scattered along the road as well. We did not have trouble with child molestation as we do today. In the fall it was not so bad. The school year began in September but I always started the last of October or the first of November because that was after all the cotton, peas, and potatoes had been picked. During the winter time, it was very cold, and there was a lot of snow. I only had one pair of shoes a year and they had to last. Walking through the snow, water and rain they didn't hold up very long. My mother would

tear up burlap sacks to shield me from the wet snow as I walked through the woods. Those sacks wrapped around your legs protected them from the snow and water. Although when I got to school, my feet would be so wet, cold and numb that I couldn't feel them. My teacher would hold each child on her lap and warm our feet in front of the potbelly stove which was used to heat the room. Of course it took almost all day for the room to get warm enough. So, we wore our coats all day and sat close together like sardines. Sometimes there were as many as sixty children in that one room. I attended that one room schoolhouse until the sixth grade. I didn't see anyone like a superintendent or principal coming to check on our condition, not withstanding the many repairs that needed to be done. No one came around to check on these things, neither did anyone come to do any repairs. This was the only school provided for the blacks to attend in that community. We were given books that had been discarded by the white school. Later, a new three-room school was built. I attended that school for two years during my sixth and seventh grade school terms. I received my seventh grade certificate at the end of the school year. Although I was needed on the farm to help pick cotton and

other crops, I still wanted to go to high school. So I had trouble attending high school. But my aunt persuaded my father to let me go to high school that year.

School days in North Carolina.
(APC)

The Community

The only social life that we had as young people was something called a "box supper" which was organized by the school or the church. The parents would cook meals and put them in a box to be sold at the school for fifty or seventy-five cents. The young men and women would sit around and if a fellow liked one of the girls and wanted to talk to her, he would buy one of the boxes and invite the girl to sit with him. My father would never let us go to the supper because it was always held at night. I would beg my mother to let me go. One day, my mother finally agreed to take me to the box supper. We walked all the way to the school, which was about five miles through the woods. Although it was dark, we weren't afraid, because nobody bothered you in those days. I saw a little fellow I wanted to talk to,

but because I was with my mother, I didn't. He didn't come to me and I dared not say anything to him. Therefore, I had no boyfriends in the community, and I wasn't interested in any. My older sister had a fellow that she met at the church. He could come to see her after church, or if he was allowed to come at night, he had to be gone by 8:30 or 9:00 p.m. My father always sat in the rocking chair on the little porch, right outside the sitting room where my sister and her fellow were. My father sat out there until the young man left. I did not know where babies came from until I was about fifteen years old. My mother always told us that babies came from logs. I remembered when my mother had my younger sisters and brothers. They were always delivered at home. When I would see her in that condition, thinking that she was having a baby, I would ask her about it, and she would tell us that one day a baby would be coming. I would go to the woods and look in all the logs. We were always sent away until the delivery was over. While I was away, I was still looking in all the logs for the baby. When we got back home, mother would say that a stork had brought the baby. There was an old lady who would come visit with my mother. Her name was Aunt Cora. I heard her say to my mother one day, "Frances, why don't you tell these gals

about babies, how they're born and so forth?" But parents just didn't talk to children about sex. I didn't know anything about sex or anything. I'm quite sure I didn't until I was around twenty-four years old, after I finished my first two years of normal school and started to work. It was during this time that I kissed the first young man who was my age. By this time, I was afraid, because I had heard that if you kissed fellows that you could have a baby. After I found out where babies came from, it was quite interesting at the time, but I kept thinking something was wrong with that, and I didn't know any better until I grew up and went away.

Cooperation and supporting one's neighbors was quite common in our community. Women saved up all kinds of scraps of cloth for a year and during the winter when all the work was finished in the field, about eight or more women in the community would come together to sew these scraps together and make quilts for bed cover. They went from house to house helping one another. On designated days, everything in the house was taken out and boiling water was thrown all over the walls and in every corner to get out all the bugs and chinches that might have gotten in over the summer. We always got a new mattress, which was made from the hay

wheat after it was thrussed. After everything was put back everyone went to the next person who needed their house disinfected.

On "corn shucking day," the corn was brought in from the fields when it was ripe and placed in a big circle. Everyone came to corn shucking night, which would continue until midnight, depending on how much corn there was. There could be thirty to forty people working. Three or four women cooked all day in big black wash pots, making stew and chicken. When the corn shucking was finished everyone would eat. People would always help each other by going from house to house as needed. Cake baking was a custom and people would see how many different kinds of cakes they could make. The one who made the most was always talked about the most. Some made as many as twenty different kinds of cakes and on Christmas week they would go from house to house, sampling everyone's cake. I don't know if whites did this or not. A few white women who always came to the store would always ask mom to bring them some cakes. When she would take them, she always had to go to the back and hand the cake to them through the door, but was never invited into the house.

High School Days

Well, the only high school near was the Harnett County Training School in Dunn, North Carolina, some forty miles away. Because of this my father still wasn't interested in my going to high school. Evidently he was persuaded and allowed me to go to the Harnett County Training School, where I went for half a year, until March. When I arrived at high school I was disappointed because I found out just how much I didn't know. I had been taught addition, subtraction and multiplication but I had not been taught about decimals, fractions, or algebra that other high school students knew how to do. As I sat in math class, unaware of what was going on, I just cried. I would stay after class and ask the teacher to help me learn how to complete the problems and how to

figure out the answers. So my teacher took an interest in me and helped me. She helped me so much and I began learning very well in all subjects. The next thing I knew it was March, planting season. At which time I was taken out to go back home and help on the farm because it was planting season. My duty was to help load the little machine with guana that was put in the earth before the seeds were planted, and to put fertilizer in the machine. I was so discouraged to have to leave school so soon, especially after just settling down and learning how to accurately complete my assignments. So once again, I talked with my aunt and explained to her that I thought it was so unfair for me to have to come out in the middle of the school year. I was so afraid I would not be able to catch up again. And I didn't know what I would do for the next year. Finally, I decided it was not advantageous for me to try to go back to the training school the next year, because it was so close to home my father would just take me out again when farming season started and I wouldn't be able to complete another full year. I spoke to my aunt, who was a teacher at the Harnett County Training School, about the problem. She spoke to Mr. Gay who lived in Enfield, North Carolina, and was the

principal of the high school there. She told him that I was very much interested in going to school and also explained the situation regarding my father taking me out of school the year before. He helped my aunt persuade my father to send me to Brigg Junior College that year. I got a job working in the dining room and helping to clean the building. That helped me to get through the year.

In 1929 there was a recession; no one had any money and banks closed down. When I returned home at the end of the year, the Depression started and I didn't know how I would be able to go to school. My father said he couldn't send me back there because he felt that I was needed on the farm, and I didn't know if I would be able to go back to school. One day I spoke with Mr. Anthony, an insurance man from Durham, North Carolina. I told him I was very much interested in going to school, but I didn't see my way because my father was not much interested because he felt that the girls were going to get married. Therefore, the boys should be educated instead of the girls. I continued talking with the insurance man about my desire to go to school and explained to him how I didn't see any way for me to go back to the Training School nor to high school. So he explained to me how it could be

arranged with me staying with families who needed girls to stay with them and work for their board as well as go to school. Of course, my father didn't want me to go because I was still needed on the farm. He also felt that girls would get married and have a husband to take care of them, but the boys had to learn so they could be providers for their families. Of course this didn't work well with me because marriage wasn't something I wanted. In fact, it wasn't even on my mind; to be honest I didn't even see anyone there I liked, let alone think about marrying.

So Mr. Anthony and I continued talking about the school in Durham and how there were families who needed girls to help around the home, especially with the children. This would give me an opportunity to go to school. He said he would speak to my father about this and he did. Of course, my father was still not so interested, but he spoke to my mother and they both decided to discuss it. At that point, I said I was going anyway. I was around seventeen years old and decided I was just going to run away from home and go anyway. So my mother talked with my father and told him of my intentions. He had an old T-model Ford in which my mother and one of my cousins took me to Durham.

The first family I stayed with in Durham was a very prominent family with two boys. I took care of the boys and learned to do little things around the house. Again I was disappointed because I was not able to go to school because his wife decided she would keep me home to learn how to wash and help around the house. One day I saw Mr. Anthony again and told him that I didn't like living with this family, because I came up here to go to school, but wasn't attending school as I thought I would. So he discussed the problem with the family and finally suggested that he would take me to his home. Of course they were not happy about that because they said I was a nice person and did very well with the boys. I then went to live with Mr. Anthony. His wife wasn't very friendly, and it was as though she didn't care for me. She just wasn't an outgoing person. Therefore, I always feared her very much. I lived there the remainder of my high school years. During that year my history teacher always rewarded us for making good grades. Usually she would give us free tickets to the movie theater. I always wanted to make good grades, because I had never been to the movies before, and I would try to answer all the questions in her class to win a ticket. When I got home I would tell the lady whom I lived

with that I had received a free ticket. The movie wasn't far from there, but she would not let me go. I had to stay home and do chores. I was allowed to go to the YWCA once a week for certain programs. So I would save my ticket until I was supposed to go to the YWCA, but instead of going there, I would slip around the corner to the movie. Before long, I was going to the movies every time I, supposedly, went to the YWCA. I wouldn't stay long but I would watch as much of the movies as possible before I had to run back to the YWCA. I hated to do it that way but I wanted to see the movie so badly. I continued doing that the whole year. I also became involved in many other activities during the school year. The Elks sponsored an orator contest. The ages were from sixteen to eighteen years old. The English teachers were asked to be available to help the students when they had questions or needed help with writing their papers. Although my homeroom teacher was also my English teacher, she didn't seem at all interested in helping me with my paper. So I asked one of the other English teachers to help me. I really wanted to win. The winner would get a very good prize and a chance to go to South Carolina to compete again. The winner in South Carolina would go to Philadelphia to compete for a

scholarship. Everyone was excited about this competition. Of course, I was very much interested in competing because I always liked to talk, so I joined the contest. After my paper was completed I began reading it over for perfection, pronouncing the words over and over while washing dishes or whatever I was doing. Each participant had to recite their topic that night before the judges. There were about ten or twelve of us in the contest and I won first prize. Of course, I was overjoyed. My homeroom teacher didn't seem to be enthused about me winning at all. Some of the other prominent people in Durham were judges. Mr. Shooler presented me with a pin which he pinned on me that night. My topic was "The Constitution and Slavery." I had studied and really worked hard on my paper and it paid off, since I was the first place winner! My next step was preparing for the competition in South Carolina. Boy, was I excited. The next day, my homeroom teacher asked for my pin. She said she was going to take it to the engravers and have my name put on it. I was so pleased that I gave the pin up immediately. I was so excited about having my name printed on my little gold pin. During the next several days, I still had not got my pin back, so I went to her and asked about the pin. She said I was

older than the other contestants who competed in the contest. I said, "Well, you had my records and you still allowed me to join the contest." I knew this was not true and unfair but I had no one to stick up for me. Another contest was held in the chapel, but I did not participate in it. Naturally, one of the girls she wanted to win, the second place winner in the first contest, won. And she went to South Carolina instead of me. However, when she got there, she lost the competition. I still believe that I would have won had I gone to South Carolina to compete against the other high schools but my teacher took it from me and I had no one to stand up or speak out against what was happening.

I kept wondering why no one would help me but I began looking at myself. I didn't have the type of clothes the prominent girls wore to such events as this. The clothes I had were clean, but they still didn't fit the criteria for the rich people. Of course, their daughters were also in this competition as well. Color at that time played a big part in our race. Also, I was poor and living with other people. In any event, she would have been accompanying me to South Carolina for the next competition and she didn't want to take me. Needless to say, the teachers really catered to those types of people.

That was something that stuck with me for many years to come; about my being out of the contest, just because I was not able to dress a certain way and because of the color of my skin. I lived with the Anthonys for the remainder of my high school years. I finished school at Hillside High School in Durham, North Carolina. After finishing high school, I didn't know what to do. So I moved out of the Anthony's home and moved in at the YWCA. They had rooms for girls to stay while attending college. I didn't know how I was going to pay rent which was $1.50 per week. Needless to say, I really needed a job. I didn't know where to look or how to find one. Someone told me about the tobacco factory. So I went to Liggett and Myers Tobacco Factory and got a job. I was making $4.50 a week and only had one bill which was $1.50 rent. Although I had a job, right away I knew it wasn't for me. The women chewed tobacco and spat on the floor. They used language that I was not used to hearing and were very loud and unladylike. I kept working, although I left the factory smelling like tobacco every day. One afternoon I was walking home from the factory and saw a girl that was in my class from high school. She was from a nice family in Durham and we used to talk at school a lot. Of course, she was-

n't working; she was going to school. She asked where I was coming from because I smelled just like tobacco. I said, "Yes, Mary, I'm working in the tobacco factory." She said, "You should not be working in a place like that; it's a very bad place." That is not the type of place for "you." I said, "Mary, I must work." She asked where I lived and I told her at the YWCA. She came by to see how I was living. Finally, she asked me to come home with her and meet her mother. She took me home with her and told her mother that she had met me in school.

Her mother asked me several questions about my family and where I came from. I told her that my father was a minister, we lived on a farm, that my desire had always been to go to school and how I came to be living at the YWCA. So, she said Ms. Mammie, I'm going to let you live here with me and my girls. She said I have girls and I never know what's going to happen to any of them because we're trying to see that all of them go to school. You can live right here and I'm going to charge you $1.00 per week. You can live here and eat here just like this is your home. When you get a job, then you can start paying me $1.00 per week. She also said that she had a daughter working at Lincoln Hospital and would see if she could get me a job there. I was

very happy. Mary and I went back to the YWCA and got my things and carried them back to Mary's house. I was so happy to be living there with Mary and her family. They were nice to me and I felt right at home. I lived there just like it was my own home.

When Alease came home, she was very friendly and also tried to help me get a job at the Lincoln Hospital. She went back and talked with them. They gave me a job putting flowers in the rooms, cleaning bathrooms and things like that. I was making $3.50 per week. Mrs. Evans said I could stay at her home for $1.00 per week. This gave me responsibility. When I wasn't working, I ate there and stayed as one of her girls. Of course, the other meals I ate at the hospital. So I stayed there for the rest of the year, making plans for going to college. I really wanted to go too nursing school, but at that time you had to go three years for nursing. Then I heard that at the Fayetteville State normal school you could go two years for teacher's training. So Alease looked into the situation and wrote a letter to Mrs. Smith, the director down there. Mrs. Smith, who was the wife of the president, Dr. Smith. He had retired, and Dr. Seabrook was the president. So, I saved up a little money to get a bus ticket, which didn't cost very much. I also had to buy a

dress or two to wear when I got there. Then I got another letter stating for me to come to Fayetteville for an interview. I went down there on the bus. When I got to the station, I only had twenty-five cents in my pocket. I wasn't even thinking about a taxi; I just wanted to know where the campus was. They explained it wasn't too far from the bus station, so I walked. I walked to the campus with the suitcase and everything I owned in it. The five miles to the school seemed much farther as I began walking. My feet began to hurt and the bag felt heavier. The campus didn't have all the buildings that it does now. There were only about four or five buildings at that time. I knew exactly where to go and went to the Administration Building to speak with Mrs. Smith. She asked me how I planned to go to school with no money. I told her that I didn't have any money but I was willing to work on campus if she would allow me. During that time, several people worked their way through college, right on the campus. This was an opportunity which was given to several boys and girls like me, who were financially unable to attend college. After we got through talking, she said I'm going to send you to another building to speak with the lady who was in charge of the work detail. She showed

me where I would be staying and what jobs would be assigned to me. My job was mostly in the laundry and cleaning the dining room. In my spare time I worked for the staff, cleaning their rooms for twenty-five cents a room. All the teachers lived on campus and this worked out good for me because I was able to make additional money right there on campus. I went to school during the day and after class I would rush right in and start working. I worked myself up to the kitchen, peeling potatoes, washing vegetables, and helping get the food prepared to be cooked. Of course, I didn't do any cooking because I didn't know how. I worked myself up to the dining room, waiting on the teachers' tables. I finished the two-year teacher's training and I received a certificate to teach.

Teaching Career

*A*fter receiving my teaching certificate, I continued going to summer school. I taught at about three schools with this certificate. The president of the college would recommend graduates to schools which needed teachers. The first year I was assigned to a school near Goldsboro, North Carolina, which was about thirty-five miles away. I received $46.00 per month, which allowed me very little money to use for summer school. Since the teachers moved to the areas where they were assigned to teach, they usually lived with the students' families and paid them for room and board. We paid between $15.00 to $20.00 for room and board per month. Of course that didn't leave much money for buying clothes and other necessities. I lived about six miles from the school, on a dirt

road. The school was a one-room house and I had to leave home early so that I could get there before the children arrived. I had to make the fire and try to get the room warm before the children got there. All we had to heat the room was a potbelly stove. I wasn't used to making fires in those stoves. Each afternoon before school was out, the children would go out and pick up sticks or whatever they could find to make a fire with the next morning. We did not have a bus to pick up the black children, but the white children had a bus which picked them up and took them home.

There was a white school not far from the black school where I taught. One day while walking to school in the rain, the bus driver stopped and asked me if I wanted a ride. There was always a seat right up front for me. When we got to my school he would let me out and keep on to his school. If I were walking alone after school was out, he would give me a ride back up to where I lived and continue taking the children home. There was no discussion on the bus; I just got on and sat down, and when I got off I said, "Thank you." I wish today that I could find him or knew where that young man was, so I could thank him again. That was a difficult year for me. The people I lived with

were very nice and they had two children. My room had a small lamp and you could not do any reading or homework by this lamp. There was no heat in the bedrooms and everyone had to sit around the fireplace until they got ready to go to bed. As I looked around at my situation, I couldn't help but think about all I had gone through in order to become a teacher and things still were hard for me. Finally I decided that I wasn't sure teaching was what I wanted to do but I continued going to summer school and continued working at the college during the summer. This was how I paid for my summer classes. One day, I met one of the other teachers, and while she and I were talking, I mentioned to her my loss of interest in teaching. We discussed going to New York, instead of teaching the upcoming year. She agreed and off we went to New York. We didn't tell anyone, we just went.

When we got to New York, there were no jobs to be found. Of course we didn't go looking for teaching jobs. I just assumed this was one of the places I would never be able to get a job like that. So we started going to the employment agency to get help in looking for jobs. I still didn't know how to cook but the girl who went with me did and she got a job as a cook for a family. I wasn't looking for that type

of job. I told the employment agent what I was trained to do and he sent me out to a family who wanted someone to take care of their children. When I got there, the lady came to the door and I gave her my papers from the employment agency. She looked at me and said, "I asked for a light-skinned girl, not a dark-skinned girl. I don't want a dark-skinned girl." I thanked her and went back to the employment agency and explained what happened. He seemed to be disturbed and said he wasn't sending anybody else to help the lady. I didn't stick around to see whether he did or not, I left. I didn't expect to run into that type of prejudice up in New York. When I got home with my friend from down south I told her what happened and she couldn't believe it either. I did get a job making $10.00 per week, but I was paying $5.00 per week to live in a flea-bag, where they had chinches and everything else crawling around. Still, that was the best I could get on the salary I was making. At the end of the year, I started trying to save enough money to get train fare back to North Carolina. I was back in Fayetteville before the next school year started. I explained to the president what had happened and he was very good about helping me find another teaching job, once he found out I was seri-

ous about my teaching career. He was able to put me in a position at the Robeson County Training School in Maxton, North Carolina. I stayed there until I got my B.S. degree from Fayetteville College.

Although we got a little increase in salary every year, we still were not making much money. I was making $103.00 per month with my teaching degree. During my last summer in school, a gentleman came by from Washington, D.C., representing the International American Red Cross. He was recruiting girls to go to the Pacific, CVS, and other countries overseas representing them. He had a conference with several of the teachers and some of us filled out applications. I didn't think I would get such a job. After summer school I went back to my school in Maxton and about two weeks later, I received a letter from Washington asking me to come for an interview. I went to Washington, D.C. for the interview and they said I would hear from them later about their decision. About a week or two later, I received another letter telling me I had been accepted to go overseas in one of the slots with the American Red Cross. I explained this to the principal and he said that he would release me if this was what I wanted to do. He hated to lose me because I had been a great asset to the school. I

was the director of the High School and Elementary Glee Club and we had won many citations. In the spring, all of the high schools would come together for one big event. I also considered myself a good teacher. The principal and I met with the superintendent and notified him of my decision. I thanked them both for the teaching position they had given me. I stopped teaching and started making plans to go to Washington. I went home to Lillington and told my parents that I was going overseas with the International American Red Cross. My mother said, "All right if that is what you want to do." But of course, my father made no comments to anything like that; he never did. I got ready and started packing. I didn't have that much money and hated to leave my family but I did not leave with a sad heart. I was just very happy to be on my way. I wasn't afraid or anything like that. I went to Washington, D.C. and was met by the Red Cross officials who were there to meet the girls that were coming to work.

We stayed at a hotel called Store Hall in Washington, D.C. and we went to the American University where the orientation was held. The job was in the area of recreation which provided entertainment for the troops while off duty. We were there also to help

them with problems they had contacting their families. We also helped their families stay in touch with them. However, when I arrived for training, the instructors had just completed one class which would be leaving for assignment. I was supposed to have stayed in Washington for two weeks with the new people who were going overseas, but for some reason, right away they asked me to leave with a the group which had already completed their training. They gave me uniforms although I had not had any training, nor had I taken any shots. They just rushed me through everything. I didn't know anyone at that time because I had not gone through orientation and had not met any of the girls with whom I was traveling. We took a train from Washington to Wilmington, California. It took us five days on this train. I don't know why it took so long, but it did. This was in the 1940's. I came through very well with all my shots, except the tetanus shot. We had to take rigorous exercises like climbing buildings and going down on the other side. This was during wartime and we went on ships that were at risk of torpedo attacks from enemy submarines. I could not take the final exercise. I had so many tropical shots that I was not able to even enjoy the five days that we stayed in Wilmington because my

arm was so swollen. The other girls went out sight-seeing and touring the city.

Just before we took the ship, we were given a pill for seasickness. I think I was about the first one that took the pill but about the first to get seasick. Because of seasickness I was not able to participate in many exercises. There were many things to be done while onboard ship. It took us thirty-one days to cross the Pacific and we stopped one time – overnight in Sidney, Australia but we did not get off the ship. I understand that they had to refuel. It was a troop ship. All we saw was porpoise; some days were nice and some days were not. We played cards with the fellows. We were not allowed to have any contact with the soldiers. There was always on deck a rope drawn separating the young women from the soldiers. We were on one side and the soldiers were on the other side. We could sit and play cards with them by reaching under the rope without changing sides. During the evenings, we did not see any of the soldiers, but we were allowed to go into the Officers' Lounge. We ate with the officers although we were civilians. You can imagine that this being my first time on the water, it seemed like a very long trip. One of the highlights of the trip was the Captain's Dinner. There were about twenty

girls, five of whom were black. Every young lady except the blacks were invited to the Captain's Dinner. Of course that made us sad, because we all were going overseas to do the same thing. We did not know where we were going until three days after boarding the ship. Then we were given a slip of paper stating that we were going to India. I really wasn't impressed about going to India because I preferred Europe or some place like that. Anyway, I'm very happy that India was one of my assignments.

India

ndia is a land of many people, dialects and religious sects. What is most interesting about India is the skillful ways in which jewels are set. The Indian craftsman is the cleverest in the world at his work. He is said to have all sorts of secret methods which are handed down from father to son because owing to the caste system every man has to practice the same trade as his ancestors. A caste is a family group practicing from generation to generation the same occupation that is completely watertight. No member of one caste may intermarry or even dine with a member of another, if so he is excommunicated. The highest caste is that of the Brahmins, who claim pure Aryan descent. They are the learned class, such as priests, lawyers, and entrepreneurs of the Hindu scriptures. The others

are mostly the outcasts who are employed to do the most menial work. Sweepers are those who do laundry and cleaning. Many things are sacred and worshipped, including a large variety of animals and plants. The cow is worshipped by all castes, and to kill a cow or eat beef is a mortal sin, which a good Hindu would rather die than commit.

After getting to India, I was very happy about the assignment because I couldn't have found a more interesting place. All of us slept in the same room. This was very uncomfortable but we made it, and we all got along very well. After meals there wasn't much to be done, except play cards. There were no black officers on this ship. When the ship pulled into port, the thing that impressed me the most were the little Indian boys diving for pennies, as they would go all the way to the bottom and come back up with the pennies in their mouth. We were met by a representative from the Red Cross and taken to the hotel. In my hotel room, there were little lizards crawling around. They told us they wouldn't bother us but whatever they landed on they would change to that color. We stayed in Bombay three days before we took a little train to Calcutta, which also took us three days. Every time we went for meals, the train would have to stop and

we would get out of the compartment and walk around to the compartment where the food was, to be served. We would eat our meal and stay in the compartment until the train stopped again. It was really a tiresome trip because the train was not comfortable. Calcutta has been called the City of Palaces. It is also the city of the worst slums in the East. It has so many people with high unemployment. In 1942 there was a great famine. Calcutta is very hot, especially in the summer, when the rich people go to the Darfeling, where the climate is very healthy and is in full view of Mt. Everest. Snakes (cobras), monkeys and peacocks are regarded as sacred and to kill one of these would give grave offense. When we got to Calcutta, we were met by a representative and taken to the hotel to wait for an assignment. I stayed in Calcutta for six weeks. We were there to provide recreation and entertainment for the troops when they were off duty. The thing that impressed me was the little rickshaw, a two-handled buggy. The little fellow that pulled the rickshaw was so small. At first, I was a little reluctant about getting in his rickshaw behind him but everybody else was doing it. It was the only way we could get to town or the market place, or anyplace I wanted to go when I wasn't on duty and had some free

time. When you paid them, they always wanted more. One day a lady from England was getting out of the rickshaw the same time I was getting out of mine. I don't know what she gave him but she slapped him so hard that he almost fell. Of course he didn't offer any resistance. We had a few words about that. You always had to watch taxi drivers, because they would always up their fares. One day, I was on a lorry and an Indian driver took me to work. Being the director at my club, I went on the lorry a lot by myself. As we were going down the street, there were ten or more Indians holding branches with fire, so my lorry just pulled to the side and I got to the window and just sat there and looked. Some came up to the door and looked in and went on about their business. It was an interesting time over there, and yet a sad time, because you could see children on the street who were just left there after their parents died. At times, you could see children sitting on the street holding each other, with no place to go. A lot of them lived under the trees, looked much older and slept on the street. Some of the Indians lived in huts and sometimes the cows would walk inside. When this happened, you didn't run them out and they would just lie down and stay as long as they wanted. If you

were in a taxi and the cow was in the street, the driver would just wait until it moved out of the way. Going to the market place saddened me very much because some of the people would be sitting around with no arms or eyes or with their hands cut off. Some suffered from the disease called elephantitus, in which the leg or foot was so big it grew like an elephant paw. They had grown so big due to the disease, a lot of them had to carry their private parts in baskets. They just sat around begging all the time and I wasn't making much money but to see the condition they were in really made me sad. I finally decided I would stop going to the market because I just couldn't take seeing the condition of the people and not giving. After working in Calcutta about six weeks I was sent up in the jungle on Ledo Road. The Ledo Road was built by a group of soldiers. When the soldiers built this road it was nothing but jungle and many soldiers were killed by snakes and other animals. There were a lot of big snakes, such as pythons which looked so much like logs that you would not know you were stepping on snakes until they would squeeze you to death. Working on the Ledo Road was quite an experience. During the summer it was so hot, especially in that area because we camped out in the jungle. The

temperature was around 124 degrees in the shade and we had to sleep in tents under nets, which made it hotter. These nets helped keep the bugs, lizards and snakes out of your bed. Everything was built tight and close. The ceilings were made of parachute materials, which was very beautiful. We got these materials from the soldiers. Four Gurka guards, who were Indian, were always guarding our tent. While staying in the jungle, we always heard all kinds of noise, day and night and the guards would often shoot in the air to scare animals away instead of shooting directly in the bushes. If the animal was wounded, he would come out looking for you. I had a tent with a small window and a door and it was divided into a washroom, a sleeping place with a bunk, and a living room.

One Fourth of July, I was assigned to go with the soldiers on a picnic in the afternoon but it was so hot that I stayed inside all morning. I was nude and didn't have any clothes on and I didn't get under the net because no one was around and the guards could not see inside. They were always assigned to the back of the tents where there were no windows. I like to sleep until the last minute and then just jump up but this particular time, I just leaned over and said, "Oh it's so hot I don't want to get up." At

the length of my bunk was a long snake. I didn't know if it were a cobra or not. We had heard so much talk about the different types of snakes. I jumped through the two doors and didn't touch anything; of course I was out there jumping straight up and down shouting, "Cobra, cobra, cobra."

Fortunately, one of the other girls was in her tent and heard me screaming and ran out with a blanket and threw it around me. The guards ran around to the front of the tent immediately, looked in the little window where I was pointing and they saw it was a cobra. It was very angry because it had its head up in a coral position. It must have been laying there for some time in a stretched out position. The officers had to shoot the cobra four times. Of course the Indians assigned to us did not want us to kill any snakes, just run them off. I wasn't about to let them run it off, I said, "Kill it and get it out of there," so they killed it and dragged it out of my tent. We were not camping with the American soldiers, but we were near them. Some of the guards heard me hollering and ran over to see what was happening but by then all the commotion was over. I was called, "Cobra Jean" for a long time after that; so anybody that will read this and know about this

story would call me that today.

It was very difficult and inconvenient being in the jungle because all the comforts we needed were all on the outside. Of course they build toilets, but snakes or anything could be in them. We had an old command car that one of the soldiers would use to take us to our assigned area or wherever we had to go. One of the drivers named Willie was waiting for us and he decided to use the outside toilet. We heard hollering and found the driver trying to pull up his pants because there was this big snake hanging from the top of the toilet, between the sacks and the ceiling. They also have different customs. I was able to meet one of the lower classes and was invited to witness one particular custom that they went through. It was impossible for me to learn all about the customs of these different classes of people in India unless I was there just to study the caste system. What I am talking about are the things that I was able to witness or observe during my spare time, while I was there. I was invited to the home of one Indian that worked in our club. I was very friendly with him, as I tried to be friendly to all the Indians. One day he said, "You come home with me." So I went home with him. His wife had been sick for some time. In this home there

were three or four people living there but I only saw one big wide flat bed; that was where his wife was laying. In order for her to get well, this is what he said they did. First the family was called in and they went through some type of ritual and so forth. The reason for that is that they were trying to run the devil out of the house. If that did not work they were going to clean and wash the whole house. If that didn't work, they would call in the witch doctor and see what would happen then. There was another custom that when people died in the home, they would take the whole bed out. This was called "burning gat." I had taken tours to this burning gat with the soldiers. They would put the whole bed on a funeral pyre—a pile of wood built together with logs, straw and branches. Then the body and the bed would be placed on the pyre. A member of the family would light a bottle with oil in it and walk all around the pyre sprinkling oil, as another family member would set it on fire. Of course there was no sadness to this ritual because people just walked around and around there until the person was burned up. It took a long time for the person to burn because they burned very slowly. I was there one time when the leg of the person being burned just fell off. Of course the fresh smell of flesh burn-

ing was something hard to take. After the person was burned the ashes were thrown in the river nearby. This was also the river that people bathed in and washed their clothes and everything else.

There was another custom in which people were thrown down in a big gully. If you were going along the countryside and saw a lot of vultures flying around and coming down, you would know that was one of the places where bodies were thrown and vultures would go and eat them. So there were many things that happened and unless one, as I said, went to study they wouldn't get a chance to learn them all. Some of the weddings were also very interesting. I had the opportunity to be invited to two. They had very nice Indian weddings. The thing that was most interesting is that the people chewed beetle nut. This beetle nut was red and juicy and made your mouth red for the wedding. After the wedding was over, everybody kissed the bride. Of course, her mouth was red also. I found that very strange but that was one of their customs. We were not supposed to have monkeys, dogs or any type of pet. I always liked pets, so I had a little dog and a bird. One of the soldiers found a little monkey along the way and gave it to me. I kept the bird tied inside my tent and the monkey was free to roam all about.

Nobody ever said anything about our having pets but one day the monkey decided to bite the maid who cleaned for us. Her name was Sophie. That frightened me because I wasn't supposed to have that monkey anyway. Willie happened to be there with the command car so we took her to one of the doctors who treated the Indians. They checked her out for rabies and everything. I was so afraid because I didn't know what the military would do if they found out I had a monkey because I was not supposed to have one. It wasn't such a big bite so she came back with us and was okay. When we got back, I sent the monkey away and he never came back. I understand that when a monkey leaves his tribe and goes back to the wild, his family does not accept it. I wasn't sure what happened to it because it never came back and I gave the dog to the first soldier that came along. I told him to take it because I was not supposed to have it. I untied my bird and said, "Now you go away." He flew away and never came back. From there, we went to the Gap, which was about three or four more hours of riding toward China. At the Gap there was a hospital where some of the doctors were preparing to leave. We had a little going away party for them. Captain Reeves was leaving and he said that he was going

to give me his monkey and at the party he brought it with him and tied it to the post. The monkey knew the captain was leaving and did not want to come home with me; so he hung himself with the rope. I never had any more pets the remainder of the time I lived over there

My assignment in India was over in July 1944. After arriving in New York from Calcutta, I had to travel by train to Raleigh, North Carolina where I was to be met by someone to take me to my home in Lillington, North Carolina. As I remember the train arrived about 6:30 or 7:00 a.m. The same little waiting room was there for whites and a hole cut in the wall on the back where blacks could get a paper cup of coffee if it were open. On this morning it was not open. I had stayed awake all night on the way down, sitting in the little dingy coach reserved for blacks, with a small light above, trying to read. I had not read an American newspaper in about two years. After getting to Raleigh, being tired and sleepy, I went into the waiting room and asked for a cup of coffee. I was told that colored was not served in here, but since I had on my American Red Cross uniform, I thought maybe I would be served in the white waiting room because the little place on the back was not open. I thought, since I had

worked in India and in the jungle of Burma where I could have been eaten by snakes and other animals that this would make a difference. Although I had done my part in helping to win the war, I still could not get a cup of coffee in the white waiting room. For a second time I was told, "We don't serve colored in here." I walked out and waited until my sister came to meet me.

France & Germany

I would like to say a little something about France because I worked there for five years. France is a beautiful place with many lovely cities. Tours, where I lived, was about two-and-one-half hours from the Swiss border and about one-and-a-half hours from Paris, where I spent most of my free time. Also a lot of my time was spent in Switzerland, where I loved to visit. Tours is a university city where the most perfect French is learned and spoken and people from all over France came there to study. I met some interesting French families there and we have remained friends for over fifty years.

Bad Nauheim was a very interesting place, where many tourists came for their health. King Saud from Saudi Arabia would come to Bad Nauheim

every summer for his vacation and bring many people, including his wives. I never met his wives, but
I met King Saud's sons, and several secretaries
while they were there. They were very interesting
people. My colonel was also interested in meeting
King Saud and his deputy, Abdul, who was interested in visiting the Service Club but had to get
permission in order to do that. The colonel, his wife
and I were invited to dinner at the Park Hotel where
King Saud rented two floors for all the people he
brought with him. This was the finest hotel in Bad
Nauheim. They would also rent all the Mercedes
they could find for transportation. His drivers were
also friendly and attended the clubs and we would
go to the Park Hotel to visit.

A visit from the Top Brass, European Theater. (top)
Greeting Martha Ray in Mannheim, Germany. (bottom)
(APC)

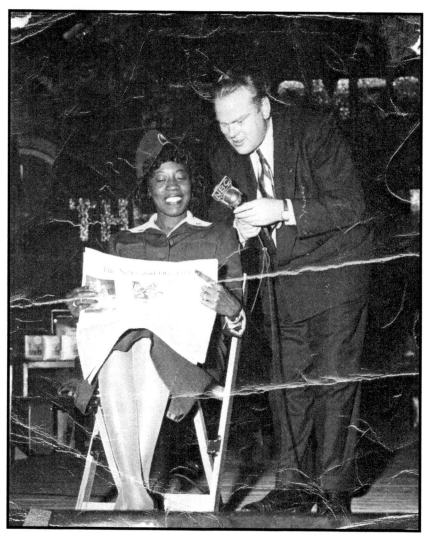

Recognition as Outstanding Service Club Director, Munich, Germany
(APC)

On tour in Nice, France in 1948.
(APC)

Feeding pigeons during leisure in Florence, Italy.
(APC)

Czechoslovakia

I have traveled in many countries and sections of Europe but the country which I found most interesting and fascinating was Czechoslovakia. When it was approved that I was to be one of four people to visit there, I began making arrangements to meet the other people in Nurnberg, Germany; some three hundred miles away. Being the end of the month, when all club reports were due, I had much work to accomplish before leaving. The eve of my departure was the only opportunity I had to pack and take care of any personal matters. After having dinner with some friends at the Officers' Club, I returned to my quarters to pack. Just as I started to place a few things together, several people dropped in to wish me a "bon voyage." I stopped packing as it was very difficult, if not impossible to

pack and talk all at the same time. The last person left shortly before 1:30 a.m. and I finished the packing that I had hardly started. At 3:00 a.m. I got into bed, knowing that I had to get up at 6:00 a.m. but being so excited about the trip, I was unable to sleep those three hours. I drove from France to Nuremberg, Germany to meet the five people who were going on the tour with me. After driving all day, I arrived at my destination and had my car put in a garage. The trip was very tiring and since we were not to leave until midnight I checked in the hotel and rested, hoping I could catch up on the sleep that I had lost the previous night. I woke up at 11:00 p.m. that evening and went down to the lobby to meet the others, all of whom I had never seen before. In the group was one other girl and two men. We left the hotel at the appointed time and started our trip "behind the Iron Curtain." We crossed the border into Czechoslovakia and after going some distance we were met by a guide who was provided to us by the government. He remained with us throughout the trip. The first place we visited, was the city of Pilsen, a world-famous beer-brewing town. Visiting the under-ground, which was part of this brewery, where the majority of the people work, would give cause for

any freedom-loving person to become sick at heart. We saw women, some of them very frail, working alongside the men, handling big barrels filled with beer. The normal working day for these people is from ten to twelve hours. It was very cold and damp, which necessitated their standing and working in water all day. They wear as many coats as they can put on and high rubber boots. The women looked very strained, but had developed big muscles from the heavy manual labor. I asked the guide about the health conditions of these people after working so long underground with these conditions. He told me that very few suffered illness by working in the brewery. Wherever stops were made, the people would stop work to come as close to me as possible. I asked the guide if the people stopped work like that every time groups of summer tourists came through. He stated that they did not, but that they were given the privilege to stop work to see me. He asked me if I objected to this and I told him that I didn't mind because everyone smiled at me. I started smiling back and continued smiling all the way through Czechoslovakia. In this brewery, we saw the whole process of beer making, from the time the "hops" are brought in, until the bottle is capped and put in a box, ready for shipping.

From Pilsen we journeyed on to Karlsteyn which is twenty-eight kilometers from Prague. Karlsteyn is situated on the left bank of the Ferounka River and has one of the best preserved medieval structures of Central Europe. This structure is a castle which never fell to a conqueror throughout its entire history. Because this castle was never conquered, its interior has been preserved almost intact. Its walls held the crown jewels of the Czechoslovakia kingdom and the German Empire. It was built originally as a safe shrine for the coronation jewels of the Bohemian Crown. Traveling through the country, mostly women are noted doing manual labor. The homes and farms are in poor condition and everybody looked underfed. Although I only saw seven dogs during my travel in Czechoslovakia, they were in poor condition, as were cats, cows and other animals. Inquiring from the guide about why there were not as many men seen working as there were women, he stated that, most of the men had to work for the state, which meant training to be soldiers and factory workers. Finally, after many winding roads and hills we reached Prague.

Prague, the capital of Czechoslovakia, lies almost in the exact center of Bohemia, on the River Ultaua.

Because of its unique architectural landmarks, Prague is one of the most beautiful cities one could visit. Not only is Prague the head, it is also the heart of the Czechoslovakia Republic. Driving through the city of Prague, en route to the hotel, I was fascinated by the beautiful architecture of the buildings, especially the state building. We reached the hotel which was situated on the main street of Prague. It was without a doubt the best hotel in Prague. Tired and hungry from the long drive, we didn't tarry outside, but signed in and were shown to our rooms. I might say of mine – a suite. Those were the kinds of accommodations that I received at every hotel in which I stayed. Although as I stated before, there was only one other girl along. I was put on a different floor. The way everyone acted, one would think that I was the most important person ever to go there. When I would come out of my room, the elevator boy would nearly run to take my handbag. At first, the people could not believe that I was an American Negro, as we were called in the 1940's. When they were told that I was, they became even more curious. Everyone that could get close to me would start asking questions about the status of Negroes in America, about the Little Rock situation and how the Negro was treated in America.

How was I able to travel and wear nice clothes? They commented that I was very intelligent and wanted to know if I had gone to school in Europe. I explained to those individuals who asked such questions that I went to school in America, was a teacher there, was working in Europe, and that I had the same opportunity to travel as any other American. I was asked again about the Little Rock situation. I told them the situation which existed in Little Rock was not throughout America, that there are sections in America, where all people went to school together and that under our democratic government and constitution, this situation would be resolved by the laws of the land. One man then wanted to know why is it that the Governor of Arkansas was able to get away with such actions. I tried to explain that America being a country of free speech and actions, he would try to get away with it, but under due process of law, he would soon be handled.

One thing I was asked by someone else was about the man who was doomed to be hanged in Alabama. When I left France and Germany, I had not seen this in the newspaper and when asked about this Negro man about to be hung for robbing a white woman of $1.98, I flatly denied that any-

thing like that would ever happen in America, especially for $1.98. When I got back to Germany and was able to get a newspaper, there it was, as big as day. Such acts and publicity as that do give America a very bad name, but what the people in other countries must realize is that everyone in America should not be condemned because of the way some act and feel. I have traveled many places during my stay in Europe and everywhere I go the same questions are always asked. When I am trying to answer some of these questions, I don't deny that some of these problems do exist in America but I do try to explain that we are making progress under our democratic government. The hotel in which we stayed had a nice sidewalk café and with the weather being so nice and warm, it was very pleasant to sit outside and watch the people go by. Whenever I came out, it would become so crowded that it was almost impossible for anyone to pass because everybody would stop to look at me and smile. The crowd became so great one day, someone put up a notice asking people to move on and not make a fool of themselves. In another section I met people from Moravia, some of whom would come and rub my skin. Instead of the guide being able to explain the points of interest to the group,

he had to explain to the people who would gather around, something about me. Many people asked how I got there, where I was from, etc. The other girl on the trip was also a Special Service Director and since our jobs were quite similar, we found much to talk about. As soon as I was alone someone would want to know if she were in America would she be so nice to me because she was white. I explained that there was not a place in America where people did not speak to one another, if they knew the person. While sitting at the sidewalk café one evening, I looked at the crowd of people which was standing there and I saw a Negro man looking at me. We looked at each other and smiled and he managed to make his way through the crowd to me. He seemed very happy to see me. He was as surprised to see me there, as I was curious to know what he was doing there if he were not on a tour. He told me that he had been living in Prague for three years and he was teaching English in one of the schools. He further stated that he was living quite comfortably and had a lovely apartment. He avoided answering questions about his family but he did say that he sought political asylum there, but did not answer any other questions. I was sent invitations to go dancing; two of which I accepted

with the understanding that my traveling companion would also be invited if she wanted to go. She was also interested in seeing all aspects of life in Czechoslovakia, so we accepted the invitations when we were told that these people were of respectable character. We were taken to the entertainment hall in Prague and we couldn't have asked for more courtesy from anyone. I met several students from different countries, who were attending the University of Prague on scholarships from the Czechoslovakia government. In discussing the educational system, as compared to American educational systems, I discovered that the students from Czechoslovakia must work all summer for the state without receiving any money for their work. This doesn't apply to students from other countries, who are there on scholarships. The state is responsible for their education and provides it free of charge. The students were interested in an exchange of music and if I would send them popular records, they would send me classical ones. The students were interested in magazines but stated that they could not receive them through the mail. My companion had brought "Life" magazine along and she gave it to one of the students, who was very happy to get it. She had to meet him outside where it was

dark so she could give it to him. He stated that he could not be caught accepting it. We took it outside, gave it to him and he rushed up the street and we never saw him again. This was the only person I met who seemed to be afraid of something.

Socialized medicine is practiced throughout the country. Health services are available to all citizens, free of charge. There is about one clinic in each district where specialists treat patients recommended by a medical practitioner. It was explained that tourists who became ill would also receive free medical care. I was told that the doctors are the best to be found in the world. Since I was having trouble with my toe, I decided to try out some of the medical care. I told the guide that I wanted to see a podiatrist. An appointment was made for me. I was taken over to a beautiful building, where about seventy-five people waited to be treated. I was taken immediately to a booth. A lady came in and my interpreter stated what I wanted to have done. First, she started cutting my toenail, and she was working at it so fast, that I was afraid for her to touch my toe. When she finished cutting my toenails, and was getting ready for the toe, I explained that my toe was so sore I couldn't stand for anyone to touch it. My interpreter gave her the

message. She looked at me rather funny but gave an indication that it was all right. I asked what she charged and she said nothing. I thanked her and left. I told the guide what happened and so he stated that the next day we would be in Karlsbad, the world famous spa, and he would get a specialist to look at it. When we got to Karlsbad I had not mentioned my toe to the guide again but evidently he had not forgotten because after dinner I was in the grand ballroom dancing, when I was paged to come to the lounge. When I got there I found the doctor, nurse, and the guide waiting for me. The doctor and nurse accompanied me to my suite where I showed him my toe. He stated that it was in very bad condition and that he would have to operate on it but I would have to remain there three or four days. I thanked him and explained that it would be impossible for me to stay. He then told me to see a specialist as soon as I got back to my station. I did see a doctor and so as I sit here writing this, I have only four toes on the foot that once had five. I was charged nothing for the doctor's visit to the hotel. In Karlsbad one sees people from all over the world who go there to drink mineral water, which is supposed to cure any ailment of the stomach or heart. Therefore, many of the wealthy people come to

spend at least one to three months a year to get the cure. The poor people who are in need of a certain operation will be sent there by their doctor and given the best treatment for nothing. Mothers are paid and given a great deal of care when they give birth to a child.

From Karlsbad, we journeyed to Marianbad, a vacation spot in which the best workers are given a fourteen-day free vacation. When we arrived there, there were many people sitting around listening to an outdoor concert. We got out of our bus and were going to enjoy a few concert selections but when we started to go down the aisle, people started to crowd around us and in a few minutes just about every-one who was seated had gotten up and joined them. I looked up to see if the concert had ended and saw the conductor had turned sideways and was trying to look at us and conduct at the same time. I do not know if he finished the piece he was conducting, but he stopped. The thing I noticed most of all was the listless, tired look of the people. The majority of them were old or looked old. Although this period of rest was free, with all expenses paid, the people seemed too tired to enjoy it. Those I talked with did have energy enough to talk about the situation in America. Education is very important to everyone

in Czechoslovakia. There are more bookstores and libraries to be found there than in any other country, unless it is Russia. There are no families without a library, no matter how poor they are. Every person buys at least three books a year. All workshops and factories have their own libraries and reading rooms. Reading is a passion and illiteracy is rare. Schools of all types are free; from nursery schools to elementary schools, technical and specialized schools and universities. Elementary school is compulsory and higher education is accessible to all who prove their ability. Those who wish to continue with studies while employed may arrange evening and correspondence courses with the same standards and the same final degrees as normal full time courses.

Marriage to Herman Fasse in Bad Nauheim, Germany, 1963.
(APC)

Herman and Jean celebrating their marriage, Bad Nauheim, Germany, 1963. (APC)

Moscow

*O*ne day while looking through some tour materials that were sent to our club by the head tour office, I saw a pamphlet with Russia written on it, with a beautiful picture of the Kremlin. I laid it aside and said I would look over the material later. After reading about Moscow and its people, it somewhat fascinated me. So after discussing the possibility of arranging a trip with my traveling companion, we decided to put in a request for free time when the tour was leaving. My friend was also a recreation worker with another military post. For an American to travel behind the Iron Curtain, which Russia was at the time, one must get approval from the IG section of the military. I inquired about the tour and was given papers to fill out. I was asked why I wanted to go there, since the

cold war still existed. When I told the man that I wanted to go in August he just laughed. I wondered why. When I got outside I asked if I had said something wrong. The man said it was just a misunderstanding. This tour was leaving from Stockholm, Sweden and I really loved that city. I had visited Stockholm twice and it really interested me that I could get another chance to go there. I filled out my application to go to Russia. About two weeks later, I received word that my request was approved but when the time came near for us to go we learned that my friend had not accumulated enough time for the length of the trip. My plans were all ok and I decided to go to Stockholm, Sweden to begin the tour. I was with strangers but I did not mind that because I was accustomed to meeting strangers and getting along with them. When I got to Stockholm and met the group, I found that it had only five men, one German teacher, who spoke Russian and four fellow students. Two were from Harvard and two were from Princeton University law school. I was not afraid of the men but I was somewhat nervous, because I did not know how they would react toward me. We met and, of course, I gave them that friendly smile and a firm handshake. It reminded me of when I was in school at

Fayetteville College and our president, Mr. Seabrook, in speaking to the student body in the chapel, would say, "Always give a person a firm handshake because it portrays much about the character of a person." I always remembered that. Those fellows stuck with me all the way and we saw what we could in thirteen days. We took a boat from Stockholm, to Helsinki, Finland. We rode all night with no place to sleep, so we just nodded. It was a rough ride but they had all kinds of food. From Helsinki, we went by train to Leningrad, which is now called St. Petersburg. We stayed in St. Petersburg for five days before we flew to Moscow. It took about forty-five minutes for the flight. We were met at the airport by our communist guide and taken to our hotel. It was a tourist hotel. People looked at me and would look at the men, as if they were wondering what we were doing there together. No questions were asked. I was given a room two floors under the men but I did not know where they were. There was a friendly lady who was always around to see what I needed. One morning before I left for the tour, the lady came to my room and said that she was the floor supervisor and wanted to know if I were pleased with the service. I wanted to say the food was terrible but I did not. She wanted

to know why I came to Russia. I explained. She wondered about a black woman traveling with a group of men. I explained. She asked if I were sent there by the state department. "No," I stated. She said I always looked nice and asked how I got my clothes. She also asked where I learned to speak good English. I told her that I went to college and earned a degree in education. She thought black people did not go to school, did not get good jobs and were not able to travel. I said, "Maam, I am black, I have a college degree, I have a good job, I was able to travel here on my own as a tourist, and I am enjoying your city." When I told her it was time for my tour to start, she looked at me and I looked at her. She left and I never saw her again.

One thing that interested me was a tour to an Orthodox Jewish Church which was very old. The men sat in small stalls like cages and had their names on them. I asked why and I was told that was the way they know who was there and who wasn't. The women didn't sit in the stalls, didn't take part in the service but sat in the balcony looking down on the service through a window. We went to a lot of different places. Everyone was scattered all around the hotel. The only time I saw the people I was traveling with was when I came down for

meals. The fellows would always look at me. Our next tour guide was a woman. The fellows were very sharp, asked a lot of questions, and sometimes made her very angry. So one day she said, "One day Russia would rule the world." I was really impressed at the way the students stood up to her. In the afternoon, we were free to do whatever we wanted to do. So the German who spoke Russian and I would walk on the back streets and saw many things that they did not show us on the tour. We passed churches, that were closed and they told the old women they were closed for repairs, so they could not get in, but they would still come every day to pray. On another walk we saw a beauty salon where they would put little coins all over your head and then wash it, press it, and then curl it. Gums was a big department store for tourists where they had everything but there was always a big line. We saw a lot of poverty there, but the children looked very well. They had pioneer camps there for children sometimes, so that when the parents were working they could sometimes stay there for weeks or months before going to school. They were always given nice clothes. One of the things that really impressed me was the Hungarian Dance Group. We got tickets for a performance but I could

not sit with the German teacher because of different ticket numbers. During intermission I was told
to come up and sit with him, so he could explain
what was going on. I told him I didn't want to sit in
someone else's seat because they had paid for their
tickets to be closer. He said that they would come
and sit in my seat. I felt guilty but that was their
custom and that is what they suggested. I stayed
there for the remainder of the show.

After the show we decided to walk to the subway
and catch a train back to the hotel but we got a ride
back instead. The people who gave us a ride were
very pleasant and they asked us how we enjoyed
the show. During the day we would go down to the
ice cream parlor where there was always a line. The
fellows would always want to go with me because,
for some reason, I would get called to the front.
They really treated me well. One day I was sitting in
my hotel room looking through some books when a
little girl came up to me and was looking over my
shoulder, as some soldiers came into my room and
observed. The book was in Russian but had it been
in English I could have gotten in trouble.

Another thing that really fascinated me while I
was in Moscow was to see Lenin and Stalin lying
there in the mausoleum. Their faces looked so

fresh. I was told that every month they were given an injection to keep them in that condition, after having been dead since 1924 and 1953, respectively. That has always stayed in my mind. We stayed in line about three hours in Red Square to see them. There were many interesting things I encountered while in Moscow. The group got along very well. We left Russia by train and it took two days to travel back to Stockholm.

After working in France for five years, I reluctantly prepared to leave. When I left France I was reassigned to Germany and was given a position in Friedburg, Germany. I was recreation supervisor at the Friedburg Service Club for three years before I decided to get married. I have not spoken very much about my social life. Of course, during the years that I had been over there, I had a very interesting social life. I met several people; some that, I thought I might have been in love with. There was one fellow in particular that I thought I loved. He was an American military man who had no family in Germany but had a family in America, which I did not know. He was a sergeant working in personnel and told the staff that if I called to find out anything about him they were to give no information. I had no plans to call inquiring about him

because I believed everything he said. During that time, one of the fellows there said to me, "Jean, you have been very good to us, doing things for us in the club and so forth. Therefore, I am going to tell you something. That soldier who just went to the states is married and he has gone there on an emergency to see one of his children." I said, "What children? He is not married." He said, "Oh, yes, he is married and has five children." Of course, that devastated me because before he left, we had talked about getting married. So he stayed in America until his time was up and then he came back. When he got back, he called and wanted to know if he could come over to see me. I said, "Oh, yes, please come right over." When he got there, the first thing I said was, "So you come back from visiting your family and I did not know you were even married." He said he was getting a divorce but I told him it would not be for me. That ended our relationship.

Then I met another fellow at that same place but found out he did not have a car. I had a car and when I worked night, I would let him use my car. He would take me to work and keep the car until I completed my assignment. I found out later that he was using my car and driving young ladies around

when I was not there. He carried on like this until he had an accident and we broke up after that. At this point, I decided that I had suffered enough in relationships with Americans. I decided to take a vacation and drove my car to Mainz to catch a ship going from Switzerland up to Holland. I just wanted to get away. When I got on that ship there were four German gentlemen across the room from me. In about half an hour, one of the waitresses came over and informed me that there was a gentleman who would like to offer me a glass of wine, which was their custom when they wanted to meet you. I said, "Thanks very much," and told her to tell the gentleman that I did not care for any. I was sitting there grieving about this soldier that I had left behind. They were not going the entire way, as they were going to Koblenz, Germany, which was about a two-hour ride by ship. About half-hour later, I looked over and this gentleman was looking at me. Of course, I returned the stare. I was not doing any flirting, although I did like to flirt but I was not in the mood for doing it at that time. I said to myself, "You big dummy, sitting here grieving over that soldier you just left and while you are grieving, there seems to be a nice person here who has eyes for you." I concluded that if he offered me another

glass of wine, I would accept it.

The ship was a recreation ship which provided music for dancing. So I said to myself, "Gee, if he asks me to dance, I am going to accept it." Believe me, in about forty minutes he did come over and ask and I got up and danced. Of course, he spoke a little English and I spoke a little German, which was enough for us to get along. We only had about forty minutes before they were to get off but I was going on to Holland. So we sat together and talked and he began to tell me about himself. He told me that every year in June they would get together to prepare for the beginning of Carnival season. He was president of the Carnival Chef Shop. He wanted my address and phone number but I was not used to dating Germans. I had German friends but not really dates. I asked him to give me his address and telephone number because usually when I am traveling and meeting people, if I am interested in making additional contacts, I usually send them a card at Christmas time. However, this was June and I really did not think any more about it. Just before Christmas I talked with Frau Rehfuss, a German woman who worked at the BWQ (a place where all the single women lived). Because she spoke English, I told her about this gentleman and

she agreed that I should send him a Christmas card because he sounded like a very nice person. So I sent the card and put my address and telephone number on it. As soon as he got the card, he gave me a call. Since my German was not that good, I could hardly understand him over the phone, so I called for Frau Reyfuss to come quickly and help me understand the call. She spoke German to him and English to me. She said that he was inviting me to his home to attend one of his big affairs in Heinbock, Germany, near Neuwied. I asked her if I should go. I told her to tell him that she and I would talk about it and I would let him know. We talked about it after he hung up and she said that I should go to the Carnival. I went to the Carnival and found that it was very interesting and the Germans were very friendly, jubilant, and happy. If you have ever been, you would notice how happy they are during this time of the year. He was so proud. He had a room for me at the hotel where most of the visitors stayed. I went to the affair and stayed there for the weekend. On Sunday he had the driver take us to dinner in Neuwied, which was about twenty minutes away. When we came back, the flower shops were closed but they had lots of flowers outside in glass cages. It started from there.

Every week after that I would get the most beautiful flowers. I set them outside my door every night
because we never slept with them in the room.
Inasmuch as, this association continued for about
a year, we became good friends and he would come
down on weekends when I was free. He also had a
friend who was a lawyer and later became a judge.
I would rent the hotel for them and just had a very
lovely time until we decided to speak about getting
serious. One weekend he was down visiting me and
before leaving he asked me to marry him. In fact,
the question was, "Would you me marry?" Of
course, I knew what it meant and was not shocked
because we had been hinting around this subject
for some time, but I was not prepared for that question. I liked him very much but I was not deeply in
love and could not see myself as a housewife. I said
that we would discuss it at another time and, of
course, when he got back home, he called me and
we laughed about it. He said he could understand
why I did not answer because of the way he asked.
I told him that I understood the question and we
would discuss it further when he came down again.
In the meantime, I discussed it with my old stand-
by (Frau Rehfuss). I did not know he liked to travel
as much as I did. We spent much time together

when our jobs would allow it. I found out that he had been widowed for seven years and he had a daughter who moved into his home to help take care of things. He was a catch for the community but he was not interested in getting married until he met me. The women asked what happened to make him fall so much in love with me. Of course I did not know anything about that but we decided to get married.

I had to resign from my job because I could not work with the State Department and be married. A month or two after that, we got married. I then moved into my first home. It was quite interesting because I told him in the beginning that I could not cook and did not clean, because I had not done that for many many years. We got married in Bad Nauheim and I met many people there. We then went to Neuwied, where we lived for three years, until we built our home in the Westerwald in the mountains. When I got there, we had a lady show me how to do some of the domestic chores. I was afraid to go into the kitchen to even make a cup of coffee; although I knew how to make coffee, I did not know how the Germans made their coffee. As time passed I learned to do many of these things. I also learned how to do simple cooking but not fancy

cooking the way the Germans did. When we had parties, they were catered and there was a lady who was always there to help us.

I was married for eighteen years and I had a wonderful husband. The only fault I had with him was that he was somewhat jealous but we were able to work through things. He loved to travel and so did I. I had already done much traveling to many countries before we married. We took many cruises to the Northland and the Midnight Sun and to different places in London and Spain. We had a wonderful life and it seems as if the time passed too fast. When he died I remained over there because my home had been in Germany for many years. I lived there for a total of forty-four years, which was a little over half of my life. I had also made so many friends and I still have them in France, Germany, and many other places which I visited while I was in Europe. I began thinking about wanting to come back to America. I always came back every two years to visit my parents, as long as they lived. Of course, this was three or four years after they passed. Although I never gave up my citizenship, it was very difficult for me to give up everything and come back to America because I lived over there for so long. It took me one year just to say that I was

definitely coming home. So in 1990, I came back to America where I now live. I enjoy being here but I still feel very deeply about Germany, because of my many friends who are still there.

Many of you I am sure have experienced some of the adversities that clouded my path, therefore, I am sure you can relate to my story. My journey was not easy, but I would not give up the experiences I encountered, while making it.

I now reside in a quiet community in Fayetteville, N.C., where I plan to spend my remaining years.

On the Rhine in Assmannshausen, Germany, 1993.
(APC)

Appendix

THE AMERICAN NATIONAL RED CROSS
NATIONAL HEADQUARTERS
WASHINGTON 13, D. C.

CHAIRMAN'S OFFICE   July 22, 1946

My dear Miss Moore:

    It was felt that the American Red Cross should
give recognition to staff members who served overseas
meritoriously in World War II. The Central Committee
as the governing body of the organization accordingly
authorized the issuance of certificates and insignia
in token of appreciation to such workers.

    The sacrifices our workers made in leaving their
homes to serve the men in the armed forces of our
country, the hardships endured, the skill and ingenu-
ity utilized in meeting difficult situations are a
matter of record and a source of pride to everyone
who believes in Red Cross ideals.

    You made a real contribution to the war effort
through your work. For your loyal and faithful service, we present to you a certificate and the emblem
of the American Red Cross which we hope you will wear
as a symbol of our appreciation.

                      Sincerely yours,

                      Basil O'Connor

                      Chairman

Miss Mayme Jean Moore
Shawtown,
Lillington, North Carolina

✚

The American National Red Cross
⟶ Overseas Service Certificate ⟵
to

Mayme Jean Moore

In recognition and appreciation of the faithful and meritorious performance of humanitarian service overseas in the Second World War as a representative of the American Red Cross

Harry Truman
PRESIDENT

Basil O'Connor
CHAIRMAN

ISSUED   July 22, 1946

City of Fayetteville
North Carolina

August 22, 1998

Mrs. Jean Fassé
1511 Londonderry Place
Fayetteville, NC 28301

Dear Ms. Fassé:

BIRTHDAY GREETINGS and BEST WISHES on this your 90th birthday celebration.

As Mayor of the City of Fayetteville, I wish to congratulate and commend you for the many contributions you have made to your family and friends over the years.

I send greetings from the Office of the Mayor and sincerely trust everyone is having a wonderful time as you are being recognized and honored on your special day.

Sincerely,

J.L. Dawkins

J.L. Dawkins,
Mayor

STATE OF NORTH CAROLINA
OFFICE OF THE GOVERNOR
RALEIGH 27603-8001

JAMES B. HUNT JR.
GOVERNOR

May 30, 1999

Dear Friends:

We are fortunate to have the wisdom, experience and guidance of our senior citizens. As Governor of the State of North Carolina, it is indeed my privilege to extend congratulations to each of you as you are honored by Norrington A.M.E. Zion Church of Lillington for a lifetime of service to your community. Your continued celebration of life is an inspiration to all who know you.

As we approach the Twenty-First Century, we continue to see dramatic changes in the demographic profile of North Carolina. Older adults now comprise the fastest growing segment of our population, and we must all be cognizant of the needs of our seniors.

Carolyn joins me in extending our best wishes on this auspicious occasion.

My warmest personal regards.

Sincerely,

James B. Hunt Jr.

JBH:sjs